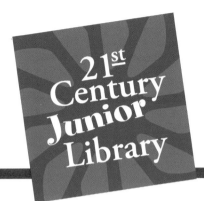

LOYALTY

by Lucia Raatma

CHERRY LAKE PUBLISHING * ANN ARBOR, MICHIGAN

CHERRY LAKE Publishing

Published in the United States of America by Cherry Lake Publishing
Ann Arbor, Michigan
www.cherrylakepublishing.com

Reading Consultant: Cecilia Minden-Cupp, PhD, Literacy Consultant

Photo Credits: Cover and page 4, © iStockphoto.com/bonniej; cover and page 6, © Thomas
M. Perkins, used under license from Shutterstock, Inc.; cover and page 8, © Mandy Godbehear,
used under license from Shutterstock, Inc.; page 10, © Blend Images/Alamy; page 12, © Hallgerd,
used under license from Shutterstock, Inc.; page 14, © Marek Pawluczuk, used under license from
Shutterstock, Inc.; cover and page 16, © sonya etchison, used under license from Shutterstock,
Inc.;page 18, © mmmm, used under license from Shutterstock, Inc.; page 20, © Monkey Business
Images, used under license from Shutterstock, Inc.

LIBRARY OF CONGRESS CATALOGING-IN-PUBLICATION DATA
Raatma, Lucia.
Loyalty / by Lucia Raatma.
  p. cm.—(Character education)
Includes index.
ISBN-13: 978-1-60279-326-2
ISBN-10: 1-60279-326-3
1. Loyalty—Juvenile literature. I. Title. II. Series.
BJ1533.L8R32 2009
179'.9—dc22   2008031777

*Cherry Lake Publishing would like to acknowledge the work of
The Partnership for 21st Century Skills.
Please visit www.21stcenturyskills.org for more information.*

CONTENTS

5 What Is Loyalty?

9 Being a Loyal Person

17 Showing Loyalty

22 Glossary

23 Find Out More

24 Index

24 About the Author

Has anyone ever said that you cheated at a game? Did a loyal friend stick up for you?

4

What Is Loyalty?

"Can you believe what Marcy said?" Kayla asked. "She said I won the game because I cheated. I didn't cheat!"

"I know you didn't," Liz answered. "You wouldn't do something like that. I think Marcy just wishes she was as good at checkers as you!"

Kayla smiled. "Thanks, Liz," she said. "You're such a loyal friend."

Sometimes we show loyalty by helping a younger brother or sister.

When you are loyal, you stick up for people who are important to you. You try to be there when friends need your help. Others know they can **rely** on you. Your friends and family know they can trust you. You take care of the people in your life.

Think!

Remember a time when a friend stood up for you. Then remember a time when someone did not stand up for you. How did you feel each time? How important do you think it is to be loyal?

Standing up to bullies can be hard. Loyal friends and family members try to find ways to help.

Being a Loyal Person

There are many ways to be loyal to your family. You can stand up to a bully who is picking on your younger sister. You can cheer for your dad at his softball game.

You can also ask about your **ancestors** and family history. Listen to the stories your relatives tell. You will find out how important family members are to one another.

Loyal friends and family members help each other.

Being loyal means sticking by people when they are in trouble. It means helping people who are in need.

Maybe your dad loses his job. You are loyal to your family when you choose to spend less money. Maybe your brother is worried about a spelling test. You are loyal when you help him study.

Ask Questions!

Is a friend or family member upset? You can show loyalty by finding out what is wrong. Ask how you can help. Sometimes all you need to do is listen.

Spreading rumors may seem like fun but can lead to hurt feelings. Being loyal means not spreading rumors about classmates.

There are many ways to be loyal at school. Maybe some kids are spreading **rumors** about one of your friends. You are loyal when you don't listen to those rumors. You are loyal when you speak up for your friend. A loyal person hears a friend's story before believing others. A loyal person keeps promises.

You can show loyalty to your school by acting
your best on field trips.

You can also be loyal to your school. You can take pride in keeping it clean. When you are loyal, you **respect** your teachers. You respect everyone who works at your school.

Does your class go on field trips? You **represent** your school when you are in the **community**. You are loyal to your school by acting your best.

It is easy to be friends when you are having fun. Loyal friends stick together even when things go wrong.

Showing Loyalty

Sometimes it is hard to be loyal. A group of people might be teasing a friend of yours. It takes courage to step in and tell them to stop. A loyal person is a friend all of the time, not just when it is easy.

What do you think will happen if you don't stand up for a friend? Will the friend still trust you? Will your friend stand up for you next time?

Do you believe that everyone should be treated the same? Then you won't make fun of someone who wears different clothes.

You also can show loyalty to ideas. Maybe you believe that people from all **cultures** should be treated the same. What do you do if someone makes fun of the way a classmate dresses? What if they make fun of the food he eats for lunch?

You are loyal to your ideas when you stick to them. You stand up to the person who is making fun of your classmate.

It's great to have a group of loyal friends!

When you are loyal, people know they can count on you. They know you won't change your mind about something just to please others. You'll be **faithful** to your family, your friends, and yourself. When you show loyalty, you just might **inspire** others to be loyal, too.

Create!

Talk with your friends about ways you can show your loyalty. Make a list of ways a friend can be loyal. Then put it where you will see it often.

GLOSSARY

ancestors (AN-sess-turz) members of your family who lived long ago

community (kuh-MYOO-nuh-tee) a group of people who live in the same area or who have something in common with one another

cultures (KUHL-churz) the ideas, customs, and traditions of different groups of people

faithful (FAYTH-ful) firm in your support of family members and friends and worthy of their trust

inspire (in-SPIRE) to encourage or influence someone to do something

rely (ri-LYE) to depend on and trust someone

represent (reh-pri-ZEHNT) to act as a symbol of

respect (ri-SPEKT) to admire or have a high opinion of someone

rumors (ROO-murz) things said about someone or something that may not be true

FIND OUT MORE

BOOKS

Klingel, Cynthia Fitterer. *Loyalty.* Mankato, MN: The Child's World, 2007.

Suen, Anastasia. *Trust Me: A Loyalty Story.* Edina, MN: Looking Glass Library, 2008.

WEB SITES

Children's Stories from Whootie Owl
www.storiestogrowby.com/choose.php
Find stories about loyalty and other positive character traits

PBS KIDS: Sesame Street— Global Grover Grooves
pbskids.org/sesame/grover/index.html
Learn more about other cultures with Grover

INDEX

A
ancestors, 9

B
bullies, 9

C
cheating, 5
communities, 15
courage, 17
cultures, 19

F
family, 7, 9, 11, 21
field trips, 15
friends, 5, 7, 11, 13, 17, 21

H
helping, 7, 11

I
ideas, 19
inspiration, 21

P
promises, 13

R
reliability, 7, 21
representation, 15
respect, 15
rumors, 13

S
schools, 13, 15
speaking up, 7, 9, 13, 17, 19

T
teachers, 15
teasing, 17, 19
trust, 7, 17

ABOUT THE AUTHOR

Lucia Raatma has written dozens of books for young readers. They are about famous people, historical events, ways to stay safe, and other topics. She lives in Florida's Tampa Bay area with her husband and their two children.